Naughty S_ _____
Recipes

It's Good For You!

Keith Pepperell

DEDICATION

To my spawn Lydia, Alex, and Jack,
none of whom are strangers to this
healthy and leafy delight.

ACKNOWLEDGMENTS

Sandon Bottom Spinach Grower's Association

Lady Estima Davenport

Muriel Dinwiddy

Sir Quimbush Merkin

Ophelia Merkin

Violet Mynnge

Tippy Tolbooth-Change

E. W. 'Lofty' Stoat

Kevin Cormorant

Spinach Scholars Everywhere

Suleiman213 - Spinach Market Image

Grimod de la Reyniere

Salvador Dali

John Locke

Terence Scully

Matilda of Tuscany

Geoffrey Chaucer

Keith Pepperell

al-Baghdadi

Bartolomeo Sacchi

Lady Joan Cumberland

Sir Francis Pepperell

Ernesto Che Guevara

Bundesarchiv - Mussolini Image

Naughty Spinach - Origins

The Middle English word 'spinach'
derived from the naughty Anglo-Norman
spinache, the Old French *espinoche,*
the Arabic اِسْفَانَاخ *isfānāḵ*), and the
Persian اسپناخ (*ispanâx*). Further,
spinach is known as *épinard* in French,
espinac in Catalan, *spanaki* in Greek,
spinaci in Italian, *španak* or *špinat*
in Serbo-Croatian, *espinaca* in Spanish

and *ıspanak* in Turkish (where the author lived and enjoyed many spinach based dishes) In medieval times spinach was often called *wortes*.

Spinach is an edible plant, perhaps the best known being spinacia oleracea, but many other plants that are eaten for their greens are also called spinach.

These include but are not limited to spinach beet, French spinach, mountain spinach, tree spinach, African spinach, South African wild spinach, Malabar spinach, red vine spinach, creeping spinach, climbing spinach, New Zealand spinach, water spinach, common sorrel, garden sorrel, perpetual spinach, chard, and naughty

Chinese spinach.

Many well-known wags and writers have had something to say about spinach:

"Fortunately I am not one of those beings who when they smile are apt to expose remnants, however small, of horrible and degrading spinach clinging to their teeth."

Salvador Dali, 'The Secret Life of Salvador Dali' (1942)

"I detest spinach because of its utterly amorphous character....the only good, noble and edible thing to be found in that sordid nourishment is the sand."

Salvador Dali, 'The Secret Life of Salvador Dali' (1942)

Keith Pepperell

"I dislike it, and am happy to dislike it because if I liked it I would eat it, and I cannot stand it."

Le Prudhomme 'Flaubert's 'Dictionnaire des idées reçues'

"There was a Young Lady of Greenwich,
Whose garments were border'd with Spinach,
But a large spotty Calf,
bit her shawl quite in half,
Which alarmed that Young Lady of Greenwich."
Edward Lear (1812-1888)

"Spinach is susceptible of receiving all imprints: It is the virgin wax of the kitchen."

Naughty Spinach Recipes - It's Good For You!
Grimod de la Reyniere

"One man's poison ivy is another man's spinach."

George Ade (1866-1944) American humorist

Like so many vegetables the origins of spinach cultivation are shrouded in some mystery.

Spinach scholars like Lady Estima Davenport suggest, "Spinach comes from a Central and Southwestern Asian gene and it may have originated from Spinacia tetranda, which is still gathered as a wild edible green in Anatolia by hungry Turks."
We do know to the ancient Greeks

naughty Romans, and other Mediterranean peoples Spinach was unknown. We also know that smart Arab agriculturists eventually found ways of cultivating spinach using sophisticated irrigation in likely in the 8th C. AD.

Sasanian Persians refer to spinach and it is argued that in 647 spinach was taken from Nepal to China where it was referred to as "Persian green."

There are works by writers in the 10th century AD al-Razi, Ibn Wahshiya and Qustus al-Rumi that contain references to spinach
In the 12th century Ibn al-'Awwam called it the "captain of leafy greens."

When spinach finally makes its way to Provence, France it soon became a popular vegetable. English Philosopher John Locke (who was shamelessly plagiarized by Jefferson) writes of enjoying spinach in his travels in France.

The Turks gobbled it down by the bucketful when prepared with meat and smothered in a delightful garlic-yogurt sauce.

When the author lived in Turkey he frequently delighted in the dish served in a little hole-in-the-wall moistening establishment in Ulus, Ankara. In Venice too, naughty Italian cooks too used advanced Arab flavorings using pine nuts and sultanas for several of their ever-popular spinach dishes. Sephardim Jews also delighted in *shpongous*, a naughtily savory of sheep's cheese on the Shavuot holiday. Further too, in Damascus c. 1250 AC, *burani* was a tasty dish of Persian origin, made with naughty local spinach yogurt, garlic, and spices. Most excellent food scholar Clifford Wright informs, "In 1614, Castelvetro calls for spinach to be used as the stuffing for *tortelli*." By the late 1500s, the largely toothless English feasted on spinach and the colonists brought spinach (although no cricket or ability to use silverware) to N. America and by the early 19th century several varieties were now quite well-established.

Lively dickering at the spinach market
by Suleiman213

Naughty spinach is loaded with nutrients and antioxidants and accordingly very healthy. Spinach may eye health, reduce oxidative stress, prevent cancer, and reduce blood pressure levels.

The Nutrition Facts per 100g of Spinach are according to USDA

Keith Pepperell

Nutrition Facts
Serving Size 100 g

Amount Per Serving

Calories 23

	% Daily Values*
Total Fat 0.39g	**1%**
Saturated Fat 0.063g	**0%**
Trans Fat 0g	
Polyunsaturated Fat 0.165g	
Monounsaturated Fat 0.01g	
Cholesterol 0mg	**0%**
Potassium 558mg	**16%**
Sodium 79mg	**3%**
Total Carbohydrate 3.63g	**1%**
Dietary Fiber 2.2g	**9%**
Sugars 0.42g	
Protein 2.86g	**6%**

*Percent Daily Values are based on a 2,000 calorie diet. Your Daily Values may be higher or lower depending on your calorie needs.

	Calories	2,000	2,500
Total Fat	Less than	65g	80g
Sat Fat	Less than	20g	25g
Cholesterol	Less than	300mg	300mg
Sodium	Less than	2400mg	2400mg
Total Carbohydrate		300g	375g
Dietary Fiber		25g	30g

Spinach harvesting

Some Medieval Spinach Recipes

Matilda of Tuscany's Naughty Medieval Spinach Pie

This delightful dish with its dusky, earthy, and delightfully moist undertones was probably first prepared for Naughty Matilda of Tuscany, who was likely the most powerful woman in the world during her lifetime and who died in 1115, in Bondeno, Italy.

Her cook Adelheid the Swarthy created a spinach dish of which she was particularly fond.

Sadly she caught a nasty cold while flogging a servant in inclement weather and succumbed.

She died without heirs and the many confusions concerning the disposition of her kitchen equipment and larder items, led to further controversy between the Pope and imperial ruler. The papacy under Pope Paschal II contended that she had willed the following spinach pie recipe to the church

Ingredients

3 cups, all-purpose flour 1 pound fresh baby spinach

Naughty Spinach Recipes - It's Good For You!

8 ounces blanched almonds

4 large free-range brown eggs, separated

1/4 teaspoon kosher or nun-blessed salt

2 teaspoons baking powder

9 ounces best salted butter, 2 sticks plus 2 tablespoons

7/8 cups granulated sugar

4 more large naughty free-range brown egg yolks

Zest of 1 Mayer lemon

2/3 cups granulated sugar

2 1/2 ounces minced candied lemon peel

1/4 cup Maraschino cherry juice

2 tablespoons pine nuts

Confectioners' sugar

Method

Crust

Keith Pepperell

In a big ol' bowl mix the flour,
butter, and sugar with clean, nicely
manicured hands until the mixture
takes on a kind of coarse sandy
texture.

Add the naughty egg yolks, baking
powder, Mayer lemon zest and kosher or
nun-blessed salt and mix until dough
forms

Roll the dough into a disc, cover and
refrigerate for half an hour minutes
before rolling the pastry out.

Lightly butter a 10″ pie dish. Roll
out 2/3 of the dough hanging some well
over the sides. Pinch extremities the
dough between thumb and forefinger
about 1/2 inch apart. The pastry will
likely purr with delight.

Poke some holes with a fork throughout the bottom and sides of the pastry.

Roll out the remaining dough to form attractive, naughty little lattices over the top of the filling.

Drink a nice cold beer and lightly flog your helper.

Refrigerate all the dough, covered in plastic wrap, until ready to use.

Filling

Cook the spinach until tender.

Allow to cool.

Squeeze out gently any moistnesses all the cooking liquids and finely chop using a handy-dandy-whipper-stick or small food processor.

Reserve.

Grind the almonds until they resemble coarse sand and Reserve.

Beat the nice brown free-range locally sourced egg yolks with 1/3 cup of the sugar until all lovely and creamy.

Add the almonds and beat until well combined. Add the spinach, candied peel, and liqueur and mix together well.

In a separate bowl, beat the whites until attractive Alpine-like soft peaks form, then add in the remaining 1/3 cup of sugar and beat well to attain a shiny meringue.

Slowly fold the meringue into the yolk mixture.

Pour into the delightfully prepared pie crust.

Sprinkle with the pine nuts and top with the remaining dough in your most artistic lattice pattern.

Bake for about 1 hour, until all lovely and golden.

Allow to cool to room temperature, then serve sprinkled with a little of the naughty confectioners' sugar.

Naughty 13th C. Baghdad Fried Spinach

This tasty recipe derived from *A Baghdad Cookery Book*, which is a translation of a 13th century cookbook *Kitâb al Tabîkh* composed by the plucky scribe al-Baghdadi.

The original manuscript, formerly held

in the library of the Aya Sofya Mosque is presently in the Süleymaniye Library.

The author visited both when he resided in Turkey.

Over time, a number of recipes were added to the originals to produce another book *Kitâb Wasf al-Atima al-Mutada*.

Ingredients

2 lbs. fresh young baby spinach
3 Tablespoons of sesame seed oil
1/4 teaspoon of kosher or nun-blessed salt
1 good teaspoon of minced garlic
1/4 teaspoonful each of coriander and cumin
A hint of a pinch of cinnamon

Method

Parboil the spinach in salted water for 3 minutes. Drain the water and carefully press the spinach to remove residual moistnesses. Heat the sesame oil in a sturdy pot. Add the naughty spinach and stir for a few minutes until delightfully fragrant, but taking great care not to burn it all. Add the lovely garlic and spices. After another minute more remove and serve. Crispy bread and a little fresh goat cheese is an excellent accompaniment together with a nice cold Turkish beer like Efes Pilsener, to which the author is no stranger.

Keith Pepperell

Matilda of Tuscany with her cook
Adelheid the Swarthy (to her right)
displaying his spinach pie recipe.

Medieval Salat with Wortes (Spinaches)

The term 'wortes' was commonly used
for all leafy edible plants but most
usually for naughty herby-plants like
parsley and cilantro, but also for

Naughty Spinach Recipes - It's Good For You! spinach, cabbage and sometimes even alluring onions & leeks.

Many medieval cookbooks advise that vegetables are often best served raw moistened and seasoned with vinegar, oil, and salt.

For example, naughty Bartolomeo Sacchi (1421-1481) known to his chums as Platina was an Italian humanist foody, soldier, schoolmaster, papal factotum, propagandist and a week-end cross-dresser who between 1463 and 1465 wrote *On Right Good Pleasure and Good Health* (*De honesta voluptate*) which was hugely popular and is often referred to as the first printed cookery book.

That most accomplished food writer Terence Scully in the most excellent

The Art of Cookery in the Middle Ages
translates Platina's claims as
follows: "What should be eaten first.
There is an order to be observed in
taking food, since everything that
moves the bowels and whatever is of
light and slight nourishment, like
apples and pears, is more safely and
pleasantly eaten in the first course.
I even add lettuce and whatever is
served with vinegar and oil, raw or
cooked."

A century or so earlier, in the iconic
Forme of Cury, appears a nice *salat* of
lettuce and herbs including *spinaches*
also often called *wortes* at that time.

Ingredients

A goodly amount (to your taste of)
Parsley, sage, garlic, green onions

(scallions) small young leeks most of the green tops removed, mint, spinach, water and garden cress, fennel, lettuce, and a little fresh rosemary.

Method

Rinse the ingredients after washing well without bruising and remove any annoying stems if necessary.

Tear rather than cut them all into smallish pieces and place in a nice big ol' bowl and mix well (but do not overdress) with a mixture of extra virgin or slightly naughty olive oil and a little balsamic vinegar and a hint of kosher or nun-blessed salt and a little ground white pepper.

Chaucer's Naughty Buttered Wortes

Geoffrey Chaucer (1343-1400) mentions *wortes* in *The Nun's Priest's Tale* (c.1390) - a later version of Chanticleer and the fox - wherein Chanticleer dreams of a sly *"col-fox"* hiding in a bed of herbs:

Chanticleer: "And in a bed of wortes stille he lay."

The pilgrims soon off on a day trip to Canterbury after enjoying a nice plate of *wortes* and a flagon of ale or two.

Chaucer did not provide a recipe for

the rooster Chanticleer because the feathered biped was probably, like dear old Lady Estima Davenport herself "one tough old bird."

The Nun's Priest hoping for wortes

Ingredients

8 cups of fresh, young, naughty spinach (*wortes*)

1/2 stick (about 2 ounces or so) of best salted butter

Kosher or nun's-prest-blessed salt to taste

1 cup favorite crisp, fresh croutons

Method

Cover the well-washed spinach with any toughish stalks removed with water; add the best salted butter and bring to a boil; add the Kosher or nun's-priest-blessed salt. Reduce heat & cook until all lovely and tender; drain. Place the crisp, fresh croutons in an attractive serving bowl and cover with the naughty cooked spinach.

De Honesta Voluptate's Blitum et Torte – Spinach Pie

Another of Bartolomeo Sacchi's (1421-1481) or naughty Platina's recipes in *On Right Good Pleasure and Good Health* (*De honesta voluptate*) appears this lovely spinach pie recipe

Ingredients for Eight Churls or Five Gluttons

1 deep-dish pre-baked pie crust

3/4 pound sharp cheddar cheese, grated

5 free-range locally sourced brown egg whites, lightly beaten

4 ounces melted best salted butter

1 pound fresh baby spinach leaves

2 tablespoons fresh basil, chopped

1/2 cup fresh parsley, annoying stems

removed and well-chopped

3/4 teaspoon fresh chopped mint
annoying stalks removed

3/4 teaspoon fresh marjoram

1 1/2 teaspoon fresh sage

1/2 ounce fresh ginger root, peeled
and very minced finely

Ground white pepper

1/4 teaspoon Kosher or nun-blessed
salt

Method

Pre-bake the pie crusts. Grate the
nice sharp cheddar cheese and mix it
with the all of the delightful and
freshly chopped herbs. In another
bowl, place the very lightly beaten
egg whites and add the best salted
melted butter. Mix this together with
the cheddar cheese and chopped herbs.

Reserve and enjoy a nice cold glass of

scrumpy (alcoholic cider). Remember
not to operate a blacksmithery or an
ox drawn heavy plough. Add the egg
mixture to the baked pie crusts and
bake until the top of the pie is all
lovely and golden and the filling is
delightfully firm. Forty minutes or so
will do the trick. Cool and serve with
a nice green salad and a bucket of
scrumpy.

A fine medieval spinach pie made with
a little naughty potato too

Sir Quimbush Merkin's 15th Century Dish of Buttered Spinach or Wortes

A nourishing, healthy high and late medieval dish was prepared with fresh spinach and herbs and served over diced pieces of bread. This version was much favored by Sandon Bottom, Suffolk, England knob Sir Quimbush Merkin at Merkin Hall when lovingly prepared by his aged cook Torville Mynnge. {See Pepperell, K., with Davenport, Lady Estima (2018) *Lady Davenport's Noble Boke off Cookry for Indolent Gentlewomen* - Recipes for Slothful Ladies of Quality}.

In the delightful Suffolk, England villages of Woollard End and Sandon Bottom many of the author's ancestors

palely loitered during the high and
late middle ages awash with scrumpy
and full from 'toe to empty noggin top
full' of nourishing pease pottage.

Perhaps the best known scrumpy had
always been brewed in the South West
but the good yeomen of Woollard End
and Sandon Bottom had kept their
special brand of this crisp apple
cider a closely guarded secret. This
had been since at least May of 1381
when a local churl called Piers the
Cooper produced the first cask.

The brewing of Pier's extraordinary
cider coincided with an attempt by an
angry agent of the Crown, a fellow
called Bampton, to collect a three
groat poll tax from the frugal locals.
Several of these thrifty yeomen
attempted to placate poor old Bampton

with a flagon or two of Pier's the Cooper's scrumpy.

So successful was the attempt that poor sozzled Bampton stumbled over Suffolk and neighboring county Essex for several days thereafter shouting out loudly that King Richard II was a cross-dressing bastard and should stick his four groats up his bottom. This of course resulted in the Peasants' Revolt.

The history of that delightful village is further evidenced by an entry in King William I's Doomsday book in which appears: "Sandon Bottom: King's land kept by cross-dressing Roger de Merkin, consisting 3 beehives, 160 rather attractive sheep, 86 pigs, 11 serfs, and 7 goats, three witches with familiars, and plump Maureen the Drab who performs a lively bob-a-nob for only a groat."

King William I is the author's 30th Great-Grandfather.

Locally grown spinach (wortes) were comman and much enjoyed in that throat of the arboretum.

Ingredients

8 cups of well-cleaned young spinach

1/4 lb. of salted best butter

Kosher or local nun-blessed salt to taste

1 cup diced crispy bread

A goodly amount of your favorite herbs and flavorings like sage, parsley, rosemary, thyme, lavemnder (very sparingly) and cilantro.

Method

Cover naughty spinach with water; add best salted butter and bring to a boil; add kosher or nun-blessed salt. Add some herbs/flavorings and cook on a gentle heat until spinach is tender; drain. Place bread in an attractive serving bowl and cover with cooked spinach.

Enjoy with a flagon of local ale and then lightly flog a churl.

Forme of Cury's Naughty Worte, Herb, and Custard Pie

Forme of Cury is attributed to The Master Chef of the author's first cousin twenty-two times removed King Richard II Plantagenet.

Ingredients

2 big handfuls of fresh baby spinach (wortes) washed and and annoying stalks trimmed

3

1/2 cup fresh parsley annoying stems removed

1/4 cup fresh basil

juice of one naughty Mayer lemon

8 nice halved free-range brown hard boiled eggs

Pastry for one pie

1/8 tsp. ginger

1/8 tsp. cinnamon

1/2 cup of green onions

1/2 cup walnuts, well-chopped

1/2 tsp. Kosher or nun-blessed salt

2 Tablespoons of extra virgin or slightly naughty olive oil

Method

Line a nice clean pie dish with the pastry carefully and nicely fluting the edges.

Pre-bake (blind bake) for about 10 minute at 350° F.

Line the bottom of the pie crust with the hard boil egg halves.

Sprinkle the halved eggs with the cinnamon and ginger.

Pull apart the spinach and add to the herbs and the green onions all together in a food processor and chop for a few seconds. Add the chopped walnuts and Mayer lemon juice.

Put the naughty spinach green mixture in a saucepan and simmer for 4 minutes.

Spread on top of the cinnamon sprinkled eggs and bake for fifteen minutes and serve with a nice bucket of scrumpy.

Keith Pepperell

King Richard II in about 1370 hoping
for a nice tasty worte custard

Thomas Dawson's Sallat of Wortes and

All Kinds of Naughty Hearbes

Elizabethan rascal Naughty Thomas Dawson wrote a number of well-received recipe books particularly among the knobs and gentlefolk of late Elizabethan England including, The Good Huswifes Jewell (1585), The good Hus-wifes handmaid for the kitchen (1594), and The Booke of Carving and Sewing (1597). By the end of the sixteenth century we find an upsurge of cookery texts. The books are sadly class-related, since many of the ingredients were very expensive and difficult to source.

Ingredients

1 pound of well-cleaned and de-stalked baby spinach leaves

5 nice free-range naughty brown hard boiled eggs, carefully peeled

1/2 cup of chopped parsley and another of green onions

1/2 head nice fresh naughty escarole

A goodly sprinkle of fresh thyme and sage stalks removed

1 cup each local apple cider vinegar & extra virgin or slightly naughty olive oil

1 1/3 tbs of granulated sugar

1 tbs. Kosher or nun-blessed salt

1/8 tsp. Ground white pepper

1 nice plump Mayer lemon and 1 naughty English cucumber

Method

Wash all the greens, drain and carefully tear into pieces.

Mix the extra virgin or slightly

naughty oil, apple vinegar, kosher or nun-blessed salt, sugar and ground white pepper.

Stir well.

Slice the lovely Mayer lemon and lovely English cucumber.

Mix with the baby spinach and herbs in an attractive salad bowl.

Toss with the apple cider vinegar and oil dressing.

Drink a nice well-chilled glass of wine.

Arrange the sliced hard boiled eggs upon the salad.

Serve cold with just a little sprinkle of sugar.

Serve slightly chilled with a bottle of nice Pinot Grigio.

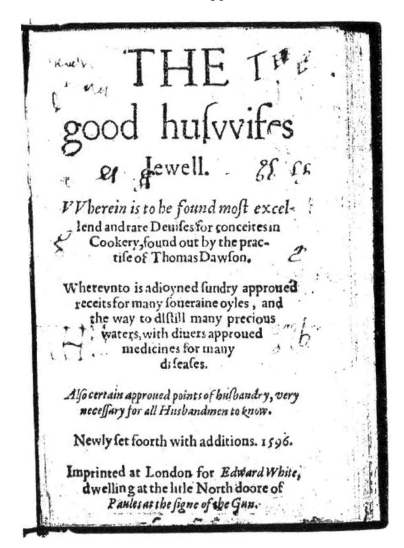

Title page from the 1596 edition of Dawson's The Good Huswifes Jewell

Medieval Persian Shula Kalambar

This tasty lentil and spinach dish was

often 'prescribed' for invalids and the sick and claimed to only be effective if the ingredients are obtained through begging on the streets.

Not an entirely healthy occupation for the sick however.

Ingredients (begged from the streets if you are sick)

6 ounces brown lentils in 2 cups water

1 pound fresh baby spinach stalks trimmed spinach

½ tsp. ground coriander

1 ½ tsp. ground cumin

1 clove of fresh garlic finely
chopped

Kosher or nun-blessed salt and ground
white pepper

Method

Cook the naughty lentils in water for
an hour until all lovely and soft.
Drain. Wilt the baby spinach spinach
in a hint of butter.

Add to the rinsed lentils and add the
spices and garlic.

Stir together with melted butter and
toss vigorously and thoroughly.

Persian Shula Kalambar

Story of the Sick Larrikin and the Cook - from The Arabian Nights Translated by Professor Quimbush Merkin

"One of the ne'er do-wells found himself one fine morning both sick and without aught, and the world was straitened upon him and patience failed him. So he lay down to sleep, and ceased not slumbering till the sun stang him and the foam came out upon his mouth, whereupon he arose, and he was penniless and had not even so much as a single dirham. Presently he arrived at the souk wherein was the shop of a cook so the larrikin, whose wits had been sharpened by sickness and great hunger, went in to him and saluting him, said to him, "Weigh me half a dirham's worth of cooked lentils and a quarter of a dirham's worth of spinach and the like of cumin, corriander, garlic, and butter. So the kitchener weighed it out to him and the good-for-naught entered the shop, whereupon the man set the food before him and he ate till he had gobbled up the whole and licked the saucers and sat perplexed, knowing not how he should do with the cook concerning the price of that he had eaten.

But he miraculously recovered from the sickness and hastily scurried away."

Some More Modern Spinach Delights

Dips are really quite nasty and spread diseases like The Black Death but some folk (usually members of the yeoman classes) favor them so let's start off with a couple of the least offensive to gastronomically sensitive gentlefolk of quality.

Aunty Rotter's Hangover Lunch or Church Social Spinach Dip

Aunty Rotter was a formidable old thing who had once beaten a handicapped person near senseless with

a croquet mallet for their having
parked in a non-handicapped space. She
always kept her pet ferret Stanley in
a pocket. She had trained it to attack
on command.

Her legendary Saturday evening soirees
in her delightful country house on the
outskirts of Sandon Bottom involved
the consumption of many buckets of gin
and she always made quiches, bloody
Mary's and spinach dips for any
survivors to gobble up the following
morning. These were also great hits at
church Socials particular at those of
Our Lady of the Ever Festering Wound
Lady Davenport and her old school chum
and companion Muriel Dinwiddy were
regularly in attendance.

Once, a team of accomplished French
trapeze artists, The Archbishop of

York, a pair of identical twin Dutch lady bicyclists on a tour of Suffolk, a lighthouse keeper, and a lively police horse, awoke with a firmness over their brows scattered all over the floor in the slightly soiled drawing room.

They later all enjoyed several of Aunty Rotter's invigorating quiches, some spinach dip, and a nice big bucket of hay.

Ingredients

2 Tbsp. best unsalted butter

1 Tbsp. extra virgin or slightly naughty olive oil

1 yellow or white onion

2 Tbsp. all-purpose flour

3 cups whole milk

1 packet ranch dressing mix

6 oz. cream cheese

1 cup Swiss cheese

10 oz. frozen spinach

Kosher or nun-blessed salt to your taste

6 pita rounds

crudité

Method

Preheat oven to 350°F.

Over a medium heat, melt the butter with slightly naughty olive oil in a sauce pot. Add onions, season with Kosher or nun-blessed salt and sauté for 3-4 minutes or until all lovely and soft and a sexy pale golden color. Sprinkle in the flour and stir until a

dry and largely desiccated paste
forms.

Slowly whisk in the whole (Vitamin D
is best) milk, avoiding lumps. Stir in
the nasty store-bought ranch dip mix
and reduce heat to low. Cook, stirring
occasionally, for 10 minutes or until
thickened slightly and while you drink
at least two nice ice cold beers.
Stir in the cream cheese and half of
the Swiss cheese until melted. Add the
spinach and remove from the heat.

Divide mixture between two small
baking dishes.

Place the baking dishes on a sheet pan
and top with the remaining Swiss
cheese. Bake for about 30 minutes

Meanwhile, bake the wedges of pita for 10 minutes or so until they are alluringly crispy.

Serve warm dip with pita chips and crudité.
Talk about Aunty Rotter's operation scars and whether elderly Mr. Fong (the little man who lives at number 23) is Japanese or Chinese. Arrange to return the horse and the Archbishop.

Aunty Rotter in 1907

Lady Estima Davenport's Spinach and Potato Dumplings with Cold Tomato Sauce

If there had ever existed a modern-day monstrous regiment of women, Lady Estima Davenport would, most certainly, have been its Colonel-in-Chief with Muriel Dinwiddy, her old school chum, senior lady's doubles tennis partner, and companion, as her able subaltern.

Indeed, immediately following the first blast of a Knoxian trumpet either lady would have instantly seized it and poked it ungraciously into the blowhard's bottom.

While preparing for their Senior

Ladies Doubles Championship at The All English Club (or Wimbledon to the less informed), Lady D would have her assistant-cook the soon to be serial murderess Janet Frobisher whip up a delightfully moist plate of spinach and potato dumplings with a nice chilled tomato sauce for their afternoon tiffin together with some petite cucumber sandwiches with the crusts neatly trimmed.

This recipe and the origins of dish are shrouded in mystery. The author claims that it was first made in England in 1353 by Percy de Mynnge the Royal Cook to his twenty-second Great-Grandfather King Edward III (1312-1377).

Seized by The Germans, and later purloined by the naughty Italians, de Mynnge's early recipe involved small pieces of swan and peacock.

Later when swan and peacock were quite
difficult to obtain the standard
recipe entailed an spinach, potatoes,
and spinach.

The original recipe was lost over a
quoits bet by Queen Philippa to
Baroness Betty 'Porky" Lorraine in
1347.

Queen Philippa was kindly woman who
persuaded her husband to spare the
lives of some folk from Calais, France
whom he had planned to execute as an
example to others following his
successful siege of that city.

She had them put into the stocks and
pelted with dumplings stuffed with
duck beaks instead.

She was interested in trade in
dumplings and Percy de Mynnge was the
first to be styled "he who is blessed

among dumplingmakes".

The Queen was a patron of the celebrated chronicler Jean Froissart who wrote, ".....this means they are bound by law and custom to plough the fields of their masters, harvest the corn, gather it into barns,and thresh and winnow the grain; they must also mow and carry home the hay,cut and collect wood, and perform all manner of tasks of this kind - including making a nice deliughtfully moist dumpling or two."

In the Royal kitchens of King Edward III flamboyant Percy de Mynnge preferred a heartier tomato sauce. During the austere times during World War II dumplings were invariably vegetarian from which they gained their unmanly reputation among 'meat and veg men'. Later the 'real men don't eat dumplings' movement was common in Texas, West Virginia and Kentucky where teeth and an elementary school education are still optional.

Janet Frobisher was well-respected in Sandon Bottom, Suffolk, England for her always delightfully moist Victoria Sponge Cakes.

Poor Mrs. Mynnge was somewhat indisposed at the time having been attacked and bitten by a swan she was attempting to place in a tall copper saucepan prior to her making some gravy with the swan's neck.

The redoubtable ladies had often been invited to the prestigious invitational event, and were keen to take on, among others, the remarkably hirsute La Touche sisters (Salomé and

Capucine-Enola), their principal rivals from across the Channel, or La Manche, as the frogs insist in calling it.

The gals easily prevailed against the unusually heavily grunting froggy old girls 6-0 6-1.

Ingredients

Kosher or nun-blessed salt and freshly ground white pepper

2 russet potatoes (1 1/2 lbs.)

6 tbsp. extra virgin or slightly naughty olive oil

1 large shallot, well minced

7 oz. fresh spinach, roughly chopped

8 sun dried tomatoes in their naughty oil, well-drained

1 large lovely fresh heirloom tomato, cored and quartered

2 sprigs fresh thyme, stems removed

1/2 tsp. Granulated sugar

3 1/2 oz. favorite tofu, drained

2 tbsp. best all-purpose flour

2 tbsp. wheat semolina flour

2 tbsp. plain bread crumbs

Freshly grated nutmeg

1 small zucchini, carefully julienned

2 tbsp. roughly chopped and nicely toasted hazelnuts

Instructions

In a large saucepan of boiling, salted water, add the potatoes and cook until all lovely and tender. Drain and let stand until cool enough to handle. Peel the potatoes rice the potatoes using your handy-dandy-ricer on a baking sheet, and then let stand to cool completely.

In a largish nonstick skillet, heat 3

tablespoons extra virgin or slightly
naughty olive oil over medium-high.
Add the shallot and cook for about 3
minutes until slightly caramelized
taking great care not to burn. Add
the spinach and cook, stirring, until
wilted. Remove from the heat and let
cool completely.

Meanwhile, make the naughty tomato
sauce: Combine both tomatoes, the
thyme leaves, and sugar in a blender
and purée until smooth or use your
handy-dandy-whipper-stick. Place the
sauce into a bowl, season with kosher
or nun-blessed salt and ground white
pepper to taste. Refrigerate for about
an hour giving you time to slip down
to the pub for a nice moistener or
two.

Place the tofu in a fine sieve and
press it through the sieve. Add the

cooled potatoes and spinach to the
tofu along with the flour, semolina,
and bread crumbs and stir until all
lovely and evenly combined. Season
with kosher or nun-blessed salt,
ground white pepper, and nutmeg and
stir to combine. Using your
immaculately well-washed and manicured
fingers , divide the spinach dough
into eighths and form each eighth into
a round lovely naughty dumpling.

Heat the broiler.
In a skillet, heat 2 tablespoons of
the extra virgin or slightly naughty
olive over medium-high. Arrange the
dumplings in the skillet and then
sprinkle the zucchini in and around
them.
Drizzle the remaining 1 tablespoon
olive oil evenly over them and then

broil until the dumplings are all
lovely and browned on top and warmed
through.

Remove from the broiler and sprinkle
with the naughty hazelnuts.

Serve the dumplings hot with the
delightful cold tomato sauce on the
side and a nice lightly dressed leaf
salad and a bucket of nice ice-cold
beers.

Benito Mussolini's Veal and Spinach Lasagna

Mussolini reading his lasagna recipe
astride his horse Big Kevin to
enthralled troops in 1929

Lady Cumberland had met Mussolini at a
social event when she was Cultural
Attache to the British Embassy in
1925, two years after he had become
Prime Minister of Italy (at the

invitation of noted cross-dresser King Victor Emmanuel III). She recalled he had been editor of the newspaper *Il Popolo d'Italia* and had written some excellent recipes in his column *Cook Today, Il Duce Tomorrow.* Lady Joan referred to him as 'a rum looking cove with shifty eyes and troubled by hot seering wind'.

Mussolini had brough some of his favorite lasagna to the event and it had been a big hit. He wrote the recipe down on a napkin and gave it to Lady Joan.

For the Filling

3 tbsp. unsalted butter
1 large yellow or white onion, minced
1 1/2 lb. best local ground veal
8 oz. naughty baby spinach trimmed

$1/4$ tsp. freshly grated nutmeg

Kosher or nun-blessed salt and freshly ground white pepper, to taste

For the Sauce and Assembly

7 tbsp. unsalted butter

3 cloves fresh garlic, thinly sliced

1 can whole peeled tomatoes, crushed by hand

Kosher or nun-blessed salt and freshly ground black pepper

$3/4$ cup whole milk

8 nice free-range local brown eggs

pasta dough (see post)

1 $1/4$ cups favorite grated Parmesan

1 lb. fresh mozzarella, thinly sliced

Instructions

For filling: Melt 2 tbsp. butter in a skillet over medium-high. Cook the

onion until a lovely golden, 6-8
minutes; transfer to a bowl. Add the
remaining butter and the locally
sourced veal; cook, stirring and
breaking up the lovely meat into small
pieces, until all lovely and browned,
6-8 minutes or one beer should do the
trick, and then transfer to bowl with
the onion. Add the palely, yet
willingly loitering naughty spinach to
the skillet; cook until just wilted,
1-2 minutes; transfer to a colander to
drain well. Carefully squeeze your
spinach dry, roughly and carefully
chop, and add to bowl with the eagerly
waiting veal; stir in the nutmeg,
kosher or nun-blessed salt, and ground
white pepper.

Sauce: Melt 2 tbsp. butter in a big
ol' saucepan over medium heat. Cook
garlic until lovely and golden, 1-2

minutes but don't burn it all !. Add
the tomatoes, nun-blessed salt, and
white pepper; cook until thickened, 8-
10 minutes, and let cool. Purée the
milk and eggs in a blender or use your
handy-dandy-whipper-stick until
smooth. Add the tomato sauce, salt,
and pepper; pulse 2 to 3 times until
combined.

Lasagna sheets: Bring a big ol' pot of
salted water to a nice rolling boil.
On a lightly floured surface and
working with 1 disk of lovely freshly
made pasta dough at a time, press and
stretch dough into an 8" oval; dust on
both sides with flour. Using a handy-
dandy pasta machine, pass dough
through machine twice, using the
widest setting. Using the next
narrower setting, pass dough through
machine two further times. Continue to

roll your dough, setting the rollers to the next narrower setting, until dough is about $1/12$" thick. Lay the dough sheet on a lightly floured surface and cut into five 12″ sheets. Working in two batches, cook the lasagna sheets for 30 seconds. Using a slotted spoon, transfer lasagna sheets to an ice bath. Place a nice dry Martini nearby

Bake the lasagna: Heat oven to 375°. Grease a 9″x13″ baking dish with butter. Lay 2 lasagna sheets in prepared dish, overlapping ever so slightly. Sprinkle 1 cup of the lovely filling over top and drizzle with half a cupcupsauce; sprinkle with quarter a cup of Parmesan, about 3 oz. of lovely mozzarella cheese, and dot with 1 tbsp. chilled butter. Repeat layering lasagna sheets, filling, sauce, cheeses, and butter. Cover your delightful lasagna with greased parchment paper and aluminum foil; bake until the filling is nicely set, about minutes. Heat oven broiler. Uncover lasagna; broil until cheese is all nicely browned, about 2-3 minutes. Enjoy with a nice bright leaf salad and a sharpish and acid dressing (blood orange works well) and eleven bottles of Chianti.

Pasta Dough

Ingredients

3 cups flour, plus more for dusting

4 nice free-range local brown large eggs

Instructions

Mound the naughty flour on a work
surface and make a large well in the
center; crack the lovely brown eggs
into well. Using a fork, whisk eggs
while slowly incorporating flour until
dough comes together. Using your well-
washed and immaculately manicured
hands, knead the dough until all
nicely elastic and smooth, 8-10
minutes. Divide dough in half, flatten
into disks, and wrap in a plastic
wrap; chill at least 30 minutes, and
it will keep up to 3 days or a naughty
weekend in Brighton.

Dr. Chittagong's Palakoora Vepadu (Andhra-Style Sautéed Spinach)

Lady Cumberland once met an elderly
gentleman from Bombay called Dr.
Pandit Chittagong. Chittagong was a

small, shiny, brown man who closely resembled the late Mohandas Karamchand Gandhi apart from his not wearing a dhoti, spinning, or sleeping with his twin nieces to avoid fleshly temptations. Dhoti wearing in the chill penury of an Essex winter gave tremendous mirth to the locals, particularly because the temperature rarely got above 37. Dr. Pandit Chittagong had a wonderful recipe for a traditional Indian sautéed spinach delight which he gave to Lady Cumberland in exchange for a basket in which to keep his pet cobra Mountbottom (in honor of the last viceroy of India).

This recipe will serve eight people or one stout lady antique dealer.

Ingredients

Quarter cup of canola oil

1 tsp. cumin seeds

1⁄4 tsp. fenugreek seeds

12 fresh curry leaves

9 cloves garlic, - 3 halved lengthwise, and 6 well-minced

1 yellow or white onion, minced

1 tsp. ground coriander

1 tsp. red chile powder

1⁄2 tsp. ground turmeric

1 big piece of fresh ginger, peeled and grated

Kosher or nun-blessed salt, to taste

3 lb. fresh alluring baby spinach

Instructions

Heat the oil in a big ol' non-stick skillet over medium. Cook cumin seeds until they pop, 1-2 minutes. Add fenugreek seeds, curry leaves, and halved garlic; cook until all alluringly fragrant, about 1 minute.

Drink a nice Indian Pale Ale. Add the onion; cook until golden brown , 10-12 minutes. Add the minced garlic, the coriander, chile powder, turmeric, ginger, and salt; cook until garlic is golden, 2-3 minutes. Take great care not to burn. Stir in the lovely spinach; cook until wilted and slightly dry, 6-8 minutes.

Enjoy with many ice-cold Indian Pale Ales and frequently toast famous Indian cricketers.

Dr. Chittagong in 1902 reclining on an early sleep number bed of nails

Serial Killer Janet Frobisher's Indian Sag Paneer

Felonious Janet Frobisher was a noted serial murderess and an adroit curry and Indian food makermaker. She was also well-known for her delightfully moist Victoria sponge cakes and thrice winning the Ernst Julius Günther Röhm

Cup Cake Challenge Trophy at the Sandon Bottom Village Fete, Cricket Match, and Hog Roast.

Her hubby, the late Sir Brian Frobisher had been Assisant-Deputy Social Secretary to The East Boreham and North Sandon Beekeeper's Association.

This turned out to be a perfect qualification for a career in colonial administration in India.

Brian's time in the Raj was entirely unremarkable, save that there was a quite famous story that did the rounds throughout the British Colonial Empire that involved both his wife, the noted serial killer Janet, and himself.

He was very fond of all manner of curries, pickles, chutneys and other

Indian delights..

It seemed that during the annual Gentleman's Smoking Evening at The Calcutta Lawn Tennis and Polo Club there had been, for many years, a competition involving a duck.

Brian, who rarely drank and behaved badly when he did, took part in the prestigious competition for several years.

Also, at the end of the evening, a number of the gentlemen present would produce their manhood and lay them upon a snooker table whereupon they were measured by a Mr. W.D & H.O Patel (second cousin of W. D. 'Chittagongfellow' Patel) a trusted clerk of the Calcutta Department of Weights and Mensuration.

The most protuberant gentleman would

have the duck presented to him on a silver salver, while a Scottish piper in full regimental dress uniform, would accompany the ceremony with a piece normally played when presenting a haggis.

He was also presented with this very tasty yet quite straightforward recipe by Col. Percy ffrench-ffrench MC. who was invariably the plucky second runner-up

Brian, by some genetic mutation, was invariably the victor.

On one occasion, when he tumbled in to the bungalow in the early hours awash with brandy, Janet was reported to have remonstrated,

"Brian you haven't been getting your thingy out at the club again?" To which Brian apparently replied, "Yes my dear, but only sufficient to win the duck."

The Frobisher's bungalow with a tiger skin rug in the foreground {killed by Brian when he hit it with a van just outside of Calcutta in 1928}

Janet was never quite sure what Brian 'did' in Calcutta, and Brian was never quite sure what he should have been doing. He did stand around quite a lot, frequently commanded slightly confused locals "as you were" or sometimes "carry on!", and at sporting events, of which there were many, he would bellow "bind and thrust!"

Sadly, Brian succumbed to a nasty cobra bite in 1936.

A rather ill-behaved cobra had slithered into Janet and Brian's bungalow and decided to take a bit of a nap under their bed.

Brian, who had misplaced his swagger stick, was groping around under the bed and hearing what he thought was the sound of a mongoose shouted to Janet "there's another bloody mongoose under the bed".

His old service revolver lay impotent in the draw of the nearby bedside cabinet still in its shiny leather holster.

Brian was soon after awarded a

posthumous gong, a Knight Commander of the Most Eminent Order of The Indian Empire.

Ingredients

7 oz. of Indian-grocery-store-bought paneer

For the Spinach

4 cloves nice fresh garlic, well-chopped

1 Serrano chile, stemmed and chopped

6 cups finely chopped spinach

Kosher or nun-blessed salt, to taste

6 tbsp. heavy cream

Half teaspoon of garam masala

Quarter tsp. of cayenne pepper

1 medium piece of ginger, peeled and chopped

Indian nannaor rice, for serving

Method - Home - Made cheese

Ingredients

8 cups of whole milk

¼ cup Mayer lemon juice

Half cup of ghee

Make Ghee

Take a pound of butter and cut it into into cubes and place in a medium-size saucepan.

Heat the butter over medium until melted. Reduce to a simmer. Cook for about 15 minutes. It will foam, bubble, go quiet, then foam again. When the second coming of the foam occurs drink a beer and toast the ghee. It is now almost ready to go. Let cool and strain several times to remove any milk solids that will differ in color from the lovely golden melted butter.

Method

You can buy paneer from a local Indian
grocery store, but you can also make
it yourself.
Line a colander with 4 layers of
cheesecloth, draping it over sides,
and set in a nice clean sink. Bring
milk to just under a boil in a .big
ol' saucepan over medium, stirring
regularly with a wooden spoon to
prevent it from scorching while
drinking several ice cold Indian
beers.
Reduce the heat to medium-low, add
juice, and gently stir until large
curds form, about 30 seconds should
see their miraculous appearance.
Pour milk mixture into colander and
gently rinse off under cold running
water any foam and residual Mayer

lemon juice from the lovely little curds.

Gather corners of cheesecloth together and gently squeeze out liquid.

Tie opposite corners of cheesecloth together to make a sack, and hang it from a large kitchen spoon suspended over a deep bowl. Set aside at room temperature until excess liquid has thoroughly drained from cheese, about 1 $1/2$ hours or a nice trip to the pub for a few moisteners.

Transfer your sack to a plate, untie cheesecloth, and loosely drape corners over cheese. Place a large heavy pot on top of cheese, then set aside for 30 minutes to compress cheese.

Remove pot and unwrap cheese. Cut into one inch pieces.

Heat ghee in a big ol' nonstick skillet over medium.

Working in batches, add the poneer
cheese, and fry until a lovely golden
brown, about 6 minutes.

Using a slotted spoon, transfer cheese
to a plate and reserve.

Save the remains of the ghee in the
skillet

Make the spinach

Place garlic, ginger, chiles, and $1/4$
cup water into blender and purée into
a smooth paste. Return skillet with
ghee to stove, and heat over medium-
high heat. Add ginger-garlic paste,
and cook, stirring, until fragrant,
about 30 seconds. Add spinach, salt to
taste, and cook, stirring often, until
spinach wilts, about 1 minute. Reduce
heat to medium-low, cover, and cook,
stirring often, until spinach is very
soft, about 15 minutes. Stir in cream,

garam masala, and cayenne.

Miss Myngge's Beef, Naughty Spinach and Egg Hash

Ophelia Myngge was the ill-educated governess of eccentric Prince Stanislavasky Kanstanti-Vasa's very plump daughter Big Olga.

Better known as 'Stan' or occasionally 'the blind Pole' he had lived in the delightful Suffolk, England village of Sandon Bottom since 1945 and umpired the home village cricket matches there.

Nobody was entirely sure what His highness's occupation was, although "something with sheep or sheep stealing" had been rumored.

During the iconic 1952 cricket season

a very special bottle, of the kind attested in Samuel Gyarmathi's 1799 glossary as *vinum adustum* or burnt wine, was ceremoniously taken down from a shelf in the saloon bar in Ye Olde Blacke Pigge Pub in Sandon Bottom and a healthy tot poured into Stan's glass. Only Stanislavasky himself ever drank from that bottle.

It was commonly understood that it was one of six bottles of Wyborowa produced by Hartwig Kantorowiczat in Poznan in 1823.

It was further suggested that all six bottles were smuggled out of Poland by his late wife The Princess Augustynka Kanstanti-Vasa beneath her copious, yet finely embroidered skirts. Her Highness was generally acknowledged to have been a woman of exceptional caliber.

Some say a seventh bottle may be hidden on Oak Island, and that parsnips were likely involved the the making of this the rarest of tipples.

Ancient alien theorists also say "yes".

His Highness was, it was rumored, a member of the Czartoryski family, had fled Poland in 1945.

He drove a battered Ford Prefect with a coat of arms emblazoned on the side with the motto *Bądź co bądź* picked out in gold in rather a slovenly hand. It seems that this liberally translates as "let be that which will be"

Ingredients

1 $^1/_2$ lb. fresh spinach - should produce about ¾ of a pound
2 tbsp. extra-virgin or slightly

naughty olive oil

1 yellow onion, peeled and chopped

$^1/_2$ lb. best ground chuck steak

3 nice brown free-range locally sourced eggs, beaten

Grated parmigiano-reggiano

Kosher or nun-blessed salt and ground white pepper

Instructions

Trim the naughty spinach, wash in several changes of water, then blanch in a pot of boiling salted water over medium-high heat for 2 minutes. Drain in a colander and cool under cold running water. Squeeze out excess water; roughly chop.

Heat oil in a skillet over medium-high heat. Add onions and cook for 10 minutes; add ground chuck and cook, breaking up with a spoon, until brown, about 3 minutes.

Add spinach, cook for 2 minutes; add eggs and cook, without stirring, for 30 seconds.

Remove from heat, stir, and season to taste with grated parmigiano-reggiano, salt, and pepper.

Joe's Spinach Spätzli with Brown Butter, Crispy Speck, and Pangrattato

Joseph Goebbels was at first a Catholic and studied the culinary arts at the University of Heidelberg under Professor Friedrich Gundolf, a Jewish pastry chef who had also made a particularly tasty gefilter fish. Goebbels had been rejected for military service during World War I because of a crippled foot - the result of dropping a huge and particularly heavy, greasy ham on it.

He had very diminutive frame, and a
pronounced limp. L I M P pronounced
'limp'.

He joined the catering division of the
fledgling Nazi party in 1922. He had
an extreme inferiority complex and
believed his sauces were always 'too
runny' and his pastries 'raw in the
middle'.

Goebbels had nothing but contempt for
toad-in-the-hole, coq au vin, pate de
fois gras, bangers and mash, and
spotted dick and as his oratorical
skills developed he gained a
reputation as a spokesman for German
cuisine. His contempt for other
cuisines in general and that of The
French in particular, together with
his complete cynicism were an
expression of his own gastronomic

self-hatred and inferiority complexes. He had an overwhelming need to destroy all non-Aryan recipes, and ignite the same feelings of rage, despair and hatred on the stoves and in the ovens of fellow Aryan German cooks.

Herr Hister, however, was deeply impressed by Goebbles' cooking skills since he used only the freshest fruit and vegetables. Goebbels employed as many as 12 food tasters for Hister. One claimed "It was all vegetarian, the most delicious fresh things, from asparagus to peppers and peas, served with rice and salads. It was all arranged on one plate, just as it was served to him. There was no meat and I do not remember any fish."

Hister's apparent enthusiasm for vegetarianism reflected the Nazi

obsession with Aryan bodily purity.
Under Goebbels' direction a Hister
Youth manual from the 1930s promoted
soya beans and spinach, which it
called "Nazi beans and spinach" as an
alternative to meat.

In 1942, Hister told Joseph Goebbels
that he intended to convert Germany to
vegetarianism when he won the war. One
earlier cook however claimed Hister "
was a fan of stuffed pigeon and
spinach and he was also known to be
partial to Bavarian sausages and the
occasional slice of ham."

Hister enjoyed Goebbels' asparagus,
spinach, peppers and peas, served with
rice and salad. Hitler it seems was no
master of silverware and one insider
later commented "Hister eats rapidly,
mechanically. He abstractedly bites

his fingernails, he runs his index finger back and forth under his nose, and his table manners are little short of shocking."

In 1939 Goebbels created a particularly lovely spinach quiche which was adored by senior members of the Nazi Party and gave Goebbels tremendous kudos and led to his appointment as Hister's Minister für herausragende Quiche Teig arbeiten (Minister for Outstanding Quiche Pastry Work).

This spinach Spätzli dish was 'borrowed' from Hister's Italian allies, prior to their retiring from global bellicose competitions in 1943

For the Pangattato

One third a cup of rendered chicken fat or olive oil
1 large loaf country bread, crust

removed, cubed

1 1/2 tsp. kosher or nun-blessed salt

1/2 tsp. ground white pepper

10 cloves garlic, thinly sliced

1 large piece of ginger, peeled and very thinly sliced

1 medium jalapeño pepper well-chopped

Finely grated zest of one half of a plump, naughty Mayer lemon

Finely grated zest of half a lime

Finely grated zest of half an orange

For the Spätzli and Serving

2 lb. fresh baby spinach well-washed and stemmed

Half tbsp. freshly grated nutmeg

1 tsp. kosher or nun-blessed salt, plus a tad more to taste

4 nice free-range brown local eggs

2 cups all-purpose flour

1 tbsp. extra virgin or slightly

naughty olive oil

3 oz. sliced pancetta

5 tbsp. best salted butter

Instructions

Pangrattato: Heat your oven to 275° F. Melt schmaltz (rendered chicken or goose fat) in a bog ol' skillet over medium.

Add bread and season with kosher or nun-blessed salt and ground white pepper; cook until lightly toasted for 7 minutes or so. Transfer bread to a baking sheet; bake until slightly dry, 18 minutes.

Add the naughty garlic, ginger, and jalapeño pepper; bake until everything is dry and lovely and crisp, about 45 minutes.

Let cool and drink a nice gin and tonic.

Transfer to a food processor; pulse
into quite coarse (or even slightly
vulgar) crumbs. Stir in citrus zest.

For spätzli

Bring a big ol' pot of salted water to
a rolling boil. Cook spinach quickly
until wilted a couple of minutes at
most.

Transfer the spinach to an ice bath
until chilled.

Drain spinach and transfer to a clean
kitchen towel; squeeze until quite
dry. Transfer the spinach to a food
processor.

Add nutmeg, kosher or nun-blessed
salt, and eggs; purée until spinach is
well-minced.

Add the flour; continue to purée until
a thick batter forms, about 4 minutes
should do nicely.

Transfer the batter to a lightly

greased bowl and cover with plastic wrap.

Reserve for 30 minutes.

Bring another big ol' pot of salted water to a simmer over medium. Working in batches, and using a colander with large holes, press batter into the simmering water.

Cook until spätzli float, about 1 minute. Stir and cook until tender, about 1 minute more. Using a favorite slotted spoon, transfer the naughty fresh spätzli to a parchment lined baking sheet. Heat a tablespoonful of oil in a skillet over medium.

Cook some chopped speck until crispish, 2 minutes or so.

Transfer to a paper lined plate.

Wipe skillet nice and clean and add butter; cook over medium until butter turns a deep golden brown (7 minutes or so should do or one nice ice cold German beer). Add reserved spätzli and toss to combine; divide between serving plates. Crumble the speck over the top and sprinkle with some of the delightful reserved pangrattato. Done and done and bon appetit!

Young German National Socialist Party members enjoying Joseph Goebbels' celebrated Spinach Spätzli with Brown Butter, Crispy Speck, and Pangrattato as they wait to march into another European country

Mr. Leslie's Naughty Creamed Spinach

Noted local nancy boy, the ever effete hair stylist Mr. Leslie Merkin, owned The Best Head in the Village Salon in Sandon Bottom, Suffolk, England.
He descended from a long line of merkin, many of whom became politicians, jockeys, animal husbandry persons, flautists, seafaring men, felons. And noted catamites.

There he did all of the knobs, including both Lady Estima Davenport and Muriel Dinwiddy - together with all of the local charity shop Godmothers and their pluckiest soldiers, including Marjorie (Slasher) Cordwangler, Agatha Flange-Gusset, and Mrs. Felicity (The Beast) Pules.

As a much younger chap, Merkin was no stranger to the Bloomsbury set, and

was a close confidante of Virginia
Woolfe, E.M Forster, Lytton Stratchey
John Maynard-Keynes, Saxon Sydney-
Turney and many others with posh
sounding hyphenated surnames.

He had also been a willing week-end
guest with his cousin the noted
poetess and welder Ophelia Merkin and
the Bloomsbury self-infatuated coterie
fueled by naughty Ottoline Morell,
whose estate Garsington was a
Bloomsbury knocking-shop of amorous
badinage, infatuation, vigorous
fingering, plenteous boy-work and not
inconsiderable gossipage.

This creamed spinach recipe was
suggested to Mr. Leslie by the late
Noel Coward, who was also no stranger
to vigorous tossing not entirely
limited to spinach and tasty, leaf

salads.

Mr. Leslie and Mr. Coward never dated.

A rather slim Noel Coward with an alleged Mr. Leslie tinkling the ivories in the rear

Ingredients

1 ½ pounds baby spinach

1 stick of best salted butter

8 tablespoons all-purpose flour

1/2 whole finely diced medium white or yellow onion

3 cloves finely minced garlic,

2 cups vitamin D milk

Kosher or nun-blessed salt and ground white pepper to taste

1 pinch ground nutmeg

3 remaining tablespoons of best salted butter

Method

Sauce

Melt 1 stick of butter in a big ol' pot. Sprinkle in the all-purpose flour and whisk together getting the lumps out.

Cook over a medium heat for five minutes taking care not to burn. Throw the in onion and garlic and stir well together, cooking for another minute or so.

Pour in the milk, whisking constantly, and cook for about five minutes.

Drink a nice ice cold beer

Spinach

Melt the other 3 tablespoons of best salted butter in a second pot.

Add the naughty baby spinach in small batches increments until all is incorporated, and cook until nicely wilted. Five minutes should be enough Season the lovely cream sauce with kosher or nun-blessed salt, ground pepper, and grated nutmeg.

Add the spinach to the cream sauce, stirring gently.

It will purr with delight.

Serve with a nice grilled steak when

still warm.

Uncle Fingers Spiro's Greek Island

Quiche

Uncle Spiro hiding out in the hills in his witness protection garb (with pipe)

Ingredients

3/4 cup chopped roasted red bell peppers

3/4 cup well diced roasted zucchini

2 cups fresh baby trimmed spinach

1/2 cup chopped and carefully pitted kalamata olives

1/4 cup chopped scallions (about five)

1/4 cup chopped fresh parsley with annoying stems removed

2 tablespoons chopped fresh mint stems removed

1 1/4 cups milk

1/2 cup crumbled feta cheese

1/2 teaspoon kosher or nun-blessed salt

4 nice brown large free-range eggs

1/4 teaspoon freshly ground white pepper

Method

Heat oven to 375°F.

Drink two cold beers while you wait

On a well-floured surface roll out

crust with a rolling pin until all

lovely and even.

Line a 9-inch plate with the fluted

edged pie crust

Line the crust with sheet of foil

Bake for 20 minutes

Drink another ice cold beer.

In a bowl, beat the eggs and milk and

stir in kosher or nun-blessed salt and

ground white pepper and reserve in a

cool place.

Prepare vegetables and herbs together

for filling.

Remove any excess moisture from

vegetable by squeezing naughtily (they

will enjoy this step)

In a bowl, add the parsley and mint

and toss together gently.

Arrange in the par-baked-crust

Pour the lovely egg mixture over the vegetables.

Sprinkle evenly with crumbled cheese.

Bake for 30 minutes or until nice and golden while you chill a nice bottle of Retsina

Cool for 10 minutes and serve with some nice pickled octopus and several glasses of Retsina

Larry 'Knuckles' Edward's Cheese and Spinach Quiche

Mr. Edwards car after taking 'a dimly
recalled short cut'.

This recipe was suggested by Larry
'Knuckles' Edwards war hero, noted
mushroom soup maker, pilot, fisherman,
hat expert, and human gazetteer, who
has spoken to every library in the
United States asking for driving
directions - few of which have
rendered satisfactory results. The
author is a great fan of quiches as is

plucky Mr. Edwards. Lots of alcohol will help the cooking time pass.

Ingredients

1 ready-to-use pie crust

1-1/2 cups shredded Cheddar cheese

1 10 oz. package of frozen chopped creamed spinach, thawed, and well-drained (frozen is just about OK in quiches)

4 nice brown free-range large eggs

1-1/2 cups half-and-half cream

Kosher or nun-blessed salt to taste

Ground white pepper to taste

Method

Heat the oven 375°F.

Drink a nice cold beer while you wait

Line a nice clean inch pie plate with the pie crust; nicely flute the edge of the crust.

Sprinkle 3/4 of a cup of the Cheddar

cheese evenly onto the bottom of the
crust; top evenly with broccoli or
spinach and remaining cheese.
Beat the lovely fresh brown free-range
eggs and half-and-half with whisk
until blended; pour over the palely
loitering ingredients in crust.
Drink another nice cold beer or
even a nice stiff Gordon's Gin and
Tonic with a twist of Mayer lemon.
Bake for forty-five minutes.
This will give you just enough
time to lightly flog a servant, an
under-butler, or a lazy kitchen
helper and also try to remember
where you left your vehicle.

Lady Cumberland's Ernesto 'Che" Guevara Spinach Enchiladas

Lady Estima Davenport and her old
school chums and tennis partners

Muriel Dinwiddy and Lady Joan Cumberland met Che Guevara in 1950 by the side of the road while the valiant ladies were enjoying a bicycling holiday in Northern Argentina.

Dr. G had just lanced a rather angry looking boil on his companion's bottom and had further notice a flat tyre on their aged motorcycle

Che had indeed got a puncture and Lady Cumberland masterfully repaired it for him, using part of her Acme Rubberized Gentlewoman Bicyclist's Saddle Cozy.

While the repairs were being completed Guevara made a great dish of his favorite spinach enchiladas that he shared with his traveling companion and the redoubtable ladies.

Keith Pepperell

Lady Cumberland enjoying a small moistener in her local, The Pig and Whistle pub

Ingredients

1 tablespoon best salted butter

1/2 cup sliced green onions

2 cloves garlic well-minced

1 package frozen chopped spinach well-thawed, drained, gently squeezed and carefully patted nice and dry

1 cup of naughty ricotta cheese

1/2 cup sour cream

2 cups shredded sharp Cheddar cheese
(or other favorite)

10 smallish corn tortillas

1 can favorite enchilada sauce

Method

Preheat the oven to 375 degrees F

Melt the butter in a saucepan over medium heat. Add well-minced garlic and onion; cook for a few minutes releasing lovely fragrances but taking care not to burn. Stir in the naughty spinach, and cook for about 5 more minutes.

Remove from the heat, and stir in ricotta cheese, sour cream, and 1 cup of shredded Cheddar (or favorite) cheese.

In a skillet warm your tortillas one at a time until flexible, about 15 seconds.

Spoon about 1/4 cup of the spinach mixture onto the center of each of your warmed tortilla. Roll up, and then place seam side down in a largish baking dish. Pour the naughty (store bought is fine) enchilada sauce over the top, and sprinkle with second remaining cup of Cheddar or favorite other

Bake for 15 until sauce is bubbling happily away and cheese is lightly browned at the edges.

Serve with a nice spinach salad and a blood orange based dressing

Sir Francis Pepperell's Naughty Spinach Balls

Sir Francis, a well-known cricketer, golfer, war hero and generally a good egg grew magnificent spinach in the

gardens of stately Cumberland Hall,
ably assisted by old Mr. Mynnge.

Out of season frozen spinach would
occasionally be used even though Sir
Francis grumbled about it.

His balls were a great favorite to the
ladies of Sandon Bottom Golf Club
where he was Honorary Treasurer.

1 package frozen chopped spinach,
thawed, drained , patted dryish

2 cups dry bread stuffing mix

3 nice local free-range brown eggs,
beaten

Ingredients

1/4 cup grated favorite fresh Parmesan
cheese

1/2 yellow or white onion, chopped

2 tablespoons melted best salted
butter

1/4 cup shredded favorite sharp Cheddar cheese

Method

In a large bowl, mix together the chopped spinach (occasionally frozen is OK), dry bread stuffing mix, nice free-range locally sourced brown eggs, Parmesan cheese, onion, butter and Cheddar cheese. Cover the mixture and chill well in the refrigerator while you play a little golf, tennis, catch a trout, or pop down the pub for a nice moistener.

Drop the mixture by rounded spoonfuls onto a lightly greased large baking sheet. Then place the baking sheet in the freezer for approximately 1 hour. When ready to bake, allow your balls to partially thaw (like a gentleman resident of the Twin Cities), about 30 minutes.

Preheat oven to 350 degrees F and lightly grease a large baking sheet and bake your balls for 25 minutes, or until lightly browned.

Enjoy with a group of elderly people while drinking heavily and complaining about social security, realtors, attorneys, insurance agents, the administration, pot smoking to relieve a bad back, young people and sciatica.

Sir Francis about to fly 'over the hump' to Burma from China in 1943

Keith Pepperell

Sir Harry Woollard's Spinach Tortellini

The author's grandfather, Sir Harry
Woollard, was a jolly old fellow with
a bald head that looked just like half
of a wonderfully brown free range egg.

He was quite a rascal it seems and had
been awfully fond of shooting and
fishing. I remember his sitting in a
great overstuffed arm chair looking
out over his herb garden with a bottle
of beer, some cheese and pickled
onions with both a fly fishing rod and
a shotgun by his side.

He had somehow managed to loose a leg.

The author remembers going to the
Chelmsford Produce and Fish Market
near the Old Shire Hall where there
was a pub called the Market House.

Sir Harry would hold court there and regale his elderly group of reprobate chums with hunting and fishing stories of yore.

He was a Suffolk man and most of the Woollards came from an area around the Suffolk village of Hartest. In the early 1500s they were mostly from West Wratting in Cambridgeshire and moved to nearby Suffolk.

He found the following recipe in the pocket of an Italian soldier whose feathered hat he had mistaken for a pheasant and accidentally shot, or so he claimed.

Ingredients

1 pound package cheese tortellini
1 can diced tomatoes with garlic and

onion

1 cup chopped fresh naughty baby
spinach

1/2 teaspoon Kosher or nun-blessed
salt

1/4 teaspoon ground white pepper

1 1/2 teaspoons dried basil

1 teaspoon minced fresh garlic

2 tablespoons all-purpose flour

3/4 cup whole milk

3/4 cup heavy cream

1/4 cup grated favorite Parmesan
cheese

Method

Bring a large pot of water to a boil.
Add the tortellini, and cook until
tender, about 10 minutes.
While you get the tortellini going,
combine the tomatoes, spinach, salt,
pepper, basil and garlic in a large

saucepan over medium heat. Cook and stir until the mixture begins to bubble. In a medium bowl, whisk together the flour, milk and cream. Stir this mixture into the saucepan along with the Parmesan cheese. Heat through, then reduce heat to low, and simmer until thick, about 2 minutes. Drain the tortellini, but do not rinse, then pour them into the saucepan with the sauce. Stir to coat, and serve.

Keith Pepperell

Italian soldiers attempting the
tactically unsound military two-step

ABOUT THE AUTHOR

The author is in witness protection somewhere in the Mid-West's grreen bean casserole belt

Printed in Great Britain
by Amazon